NOW I GET IT

Now I Get It

Inspirations for Life

JULIE TEDESCO, LPC

Cover & Book Design by Words by Jen (Branford, CT)

ISBN 978-0-578-71155-3

Printed in the U.S.A.

"I have always loved quotes and images. I find them to be inspiring and they help me make sense of the world — frequently nodding my head *ah, now I get it*. I think they help others, too, which is why I'm always sharing them with friends and family and people at work. This book evolved because I like to help people, and I thought that by sharing some of my favorite quotes, maybe I could help change a thought, an outlook, or make someone's life a bit easier."

— JULIE TEDESCO, LPC

QUOTES

The Road Not Taken

Two roads diverged in a yellow wood,
And sorry I could not travel both
And be one traveler, long I stood
And looked down one as far as I could
To where it bent in the undergrowth;

Then took the other, as just as fair,
And having perhaps the better claim,
Because it was grassy and wanted wear;
Though as for that the passing there
Had worn them really about the same,

And both that morning equally lay
In leaves no step had trodden black.
Oh, I kept the first for another day!
Yet knowing how way leads on to way,
I doubted if I should ever come back.

I shall be telling this with a sigh
Somewhere ages and ages hence:
Two roads diverged in a wood, and I—
I took the one less traveled by,
And that has made all the difference.

— ROBERT FROST

Attitudes

The longer I live, the more I realize the importance of choosing the right attitude in life. Attitude is more important than facts. It is more important than your past; more important than your education or your financial situation; more important than your circumstances, your successes, or your failures; more important than what other people think or say or do. It is more important than your appearance, your giftedness, or your skills. It will make or break a company. It will cause a church to soar or sink. It will make the difference between a happy home or a miserable home. You have a choice each day regarding the attitude you will embrace.

Life is like a violin. You can focus on the broken strings that dangle, or you can play your life's melody on the one that remains. You cannot change the years that have passed, nor can you change the daily tick of the clock. You cannot change the pace of your march toward your death. You cannot change the decisions or reactions of other people. And you certainly cannot change the inevitable. Those are strings that dangle! What you <u>can</u> do is play on the one string that remains — your attitude.

— CHARLES R. SWINDOLL

Believe in Yourself

Believe in yourself
To the depth of your being
Nourish the talents
Your spirit is freeing

Know in your heart
When the going gets slow
That your faith in yourself
Will continue to grow

Don't forfeit ambition
When others may doubt
It's your life to live
You must live it throughout

Learn from your errors
Don't dwell in the past
Never withdraw
From a world that is vast

Believe in yourself
Find the best that is you
Let your spirit prevail
Steer a course that is true

— BRUCE B. WILMER

There are three Cs in life:
choice, chance, change.
You must make a choice
to take a chance,
or your life will never change.

— ZIG ZIGLAR

We always have a choice.

We can become bitter

or we can choose to become

bigger and better people.

When we learn to recognize

that every experience can

bring a blessing of some kind,

our upset is softened.

— JOHN MARKS TEMPLETON

Life isn't about sheltering
from the storm. It's about
learning to dance in the rain.

— SHERRILYN KENYON

If we don't change, we don't grow.
If we don't grow, we aren't really living.

— GAIL SHEEHY

A goal is a dream with a deadline.

— NAPOLEON HILL

When one door of happiness
closes, another opens; but often
we look so long at the closed
door that we do not see the one
which has been opened for us.

— HELEN KELLER

It's not who you are that holds you back,

it's who you think you're not.

— DENIS WAITLEY

H.O.P.E.
Hold On Pain Ends

OR

H.O.P.E.
Hold Onto Positive Energy

— JULIE TEDESCO

Self-Esteem

I AM ME. In all the world, there is no one else exactly like me. Everything that comes out of me is authentically me. Because I alone chose it – I own everything about me: my body, my feelings, my mouth, my voice, all my actions, whether they be to others or to myself. I own my fantasies, my dreams, my hopes, my fears – I own all my triumphs and successes, all my failures and mistakes. Because I own all of me, I can become intimately acquainted with me – by so doing I can love me and be friendly with me in all my parts. I know there are aspects about myself that puzzle me, and other aspects that I do not know – but as long as I am friendly and loving to myself, I can courageously and hopefully look for solutions to the puzzles. And for ways to find out more about me. However I look and sound, whatever I say and do, and whatever I think and feel at a given moment in time is authentically me. If later some parts of how I looked, sounded, thought and felt turn out to be unfitting, I can discard that which is unfitting, keep the rest, and invent something new for that which I discarded. I can see, hear, feel, think, say, and do. I have the tools to survive, to be close to others, to be productive, to make sense and order out of the world of people and things outside of me. I own me, and therefore I can engineer me. I am me and I AM OKAY.

— VIRGINIA SATIR

We learn from the past;
it is a place of reference
not a place of residence.

— JULIE TEDESCO

The reality is that beginnings are often disguised as painful endings. So when you know that there's a constant beyond the present moment's disappointment, you can sense that "This too shall pass" — it always has and always will. When you change the way you look at things, the things you look at change!

— WAYNE DYER

Life isn't about finding yourself

it's about creating yourself.

— GEORGE BERNARD SHAW

Life is ten percent what happens to you
and ninety percent how you respond to it.

— LOU HOLTZ

Let perseverance be your engine and hope your fuel.

— H. JACKSON BROWN, JR.

Every problem is an
opportunity in disguise.

— JOHN ADAMS

The sure way to miss success
is to miss the opportunity.

— VICTOR CHASLES

PAIN

Positive Attitude Is Necessary

— JULIE TEDESCO

Life happens the way it is supposed

to, not how we try to control it.

—— JULIE TEDESCO

Resilience is about believing
in yourself, and trusting your
own wisdom rather than being
swayed by the opinions of
others.

— JONATHAN LOCKWOOD HUIE

The more you believe in your own ability to
succeed, the more likely it is that you will.

— SHAWN ACHOR

You cannot receive what is coming your way
if you are holding onto something you shouldn't be.

— JULIE TEDESCO

You must be willing to release worn-out thoughts, habits, and situations in order to receive and put to use the information Spirit will bring to you. Be patient and be open to receive the guidance that will support your spiritual growth.

— IYANLA VANZANT

When you're going through a
storm, sometimes it seems like
God is too far away, but he is
the one who is carrying you
through the storm. Just trust in
him because the sun will shine
again.

— KATRINA SMARTLOVE

TIME

Time Is Mentally Exhausting

— JULIE TEDESCO

Imagine there is a bank account that credits your account each morning with $86,400. It carries over no balance from day to day. Every evening the bank deletes whatever part of the balance you failed to use during the day. What would you do? Draw out every cent, of course! Each of us has such a bank. Its name is time. Every morning, God credits you 86,400 seconds. Every night, He writes off as lost whatever you failed to invest to a good purpose. He carries over no balance in this time bank. He allows no overdraft. Each day his grace opens a new account for you. Each night the remains of the day disappear forever. If you fail to use the day's deposits, the loss is yours. And there's no drawing against the deposit of tomorrow. I must live in the present on today's deposits; invest it so as to get from it the utmost in health, joy, and blessing. The clock is running.

— LARRY BRINEY

There comes a time in life
when you walk away from all
the drama and people who
create it. Surround yourself
with people who make you
laugh, forget the bad and focus
on the good. Love the people
who treat you right. Pray for
the ones who don't. Life is too
short to be anything but happy.
Falling down is part of life,
getting back up is living.

— JOSÉ N. HARRIS

LIFE

Life Is Full of Experiences.
Embrace them!

— JULIE TEDESCO

Bibliography

Quotes have been attributed to original sources and source material with all due diligence, including the following published pieces.

"Attitudes," ©1981, 2012 by Charles R. Swindoll, Inc.

Achor, Shawn. *The Happiness Advantage: How a Positive Brain Fuels Success in Work and Life*. United States: Crown, 2010.

Achor, Shawn. *The Happiness Advantage: The Seven Principles of Positive Psychology that Fuel Success and Performance at Work*. United Kingdom: Crown Business, 2010.

Briney, Larry. *Daily Grace for the Daily Grind*. N.p.: Xulon Press, Incorporated, 2004.

Dyer, Dr Wayne W. *Change Your Thoughts-Change Your Life*. N.p.: Read How You Want, 2009.

Frost, Robert. *The Road Not Taken: A Selection of Robert Frost's Poems*. New York: H. Holt and Co, 1991. Print.

Keller, Helen. *The Open Door*. United States: Doubleday, 1957.

Kenyon, Sherrilyn. *Acheron*. United States: St. Martin's Publishing Group, 2009.

Quotes & Quips: Insights on Living the 7 Habits. United States: Franklin Covey Company, 1996.

Satir, Virginia., Dengo, Monica. *Self Esteem* (Hardcover). United States: Ten Speed Press, 2001.

SmartLove, Katrina. *How I'm Victorious.* N.p.: Xlibris US, 2015.

Templeton, John. *Wisdom From World Religions: Pathways Toward Heaven On Earth.* United States: Templeton Press, 2002.

Wilmer, Bruce B.. *Believe in Yourself: Poems of Purpose.* N.p.: Wilmer Graphics, Incorporated, 1998.

Photo Credits

The Road Not Taken	Josh Hild
Attitudes	Tracen
Believe in Yourself	PhotoMIX Company
Choices, Chances, Changes	Vicky Tran
Life isn't about sheltering...	Aleksandar Pasaric
We always have a choice...	Kim van Vuuren
If we don't change, we don't grow...	Ben Cheung
A goal is a dream ...	Elina Sazonova
When one door of happiness closes...	Dmitry Zvolskiy
It's not who you are that holds you back...	Josh Hild
Hold on Pain Ends	Pixababy
Self-Esteem	Eric Torres
The reality is that beginnings are often...	Arthur Ogleznev
Life isn't about finding yourself	Louis
Life is ten percent what happens to you ...	Nick Bondarev
Let perseverance be your engine ...	Mohan Reddy Atalu
Every problem...	Polina Zimmerman
The sure way to miss success...	Elly
Positive Attitude Is Necessary	Cottonbro
Resilience is about believing in yourself...	Vural Yavas
The more you believe in your own ability...	Suliman Sallehi
You cannot receive what is coming	thevibrantmachine
You must be willing...	Isaque Pereira
When you're going through a storm...	Guilherme Rossi
Imagine there is a bank account...	Oladimeji Ajegbile
There comes a time in life ...	Cottonbro
Life Is Full of Experiences. ...	Jill Wellington

About the Author

Julie Tedesco, LPC, has been in the mental health field for over 20 years and has maintained a private practice in Connecticut since 2014. She works with adults and teens, and provides individual therapy, couples or relationship counseling, family therapy, career counseling, and mindfulness training. She  supports individuals dealing with addiction, anorexia, bipolar disorder, domestic abuse, domestic violence, PTSD, self esteem issues, sexual abuse, substance abuse, and trauma. Julie's training includes Cognitive Behavioral Therapy (CBT), Mindfulness Therapy, Solution-Focused Therapy, Trauma-Focused Therapy, and Conflict Resolution. Julie has acted as an Adult Advocate for sexual assault survivors and as a Family Violence Victim Advocate for survivors of domestic violence. She provides support for people on probation, parole and court-ordered oversight, has conducted forensic evaluations on parolees to identify needs, and acted as a supervising case manager for a community service social justice agency.

For more information, visit www.julietedescolpc.com.

CPSIA information can be obtained
at www.ICGtesting.com
Printed in the USA
LVHW070854051020
667930LV00005B/110

9 780578 711553